Manifest the Business of Your Dreams

100 Days of Positive Affirmations and Self-Reflections for Successful Entrepreneurs

Manifest the Business of Your Dreams

100 Days of Positive Affirmations and Self-Reflections for Successful Entrepreneurs

Janay Price, MSW, LCSW

Ordering Information:

Orders by U.S. trade bookstores and wholesalers. Quantity sales. Special discounts are available on quantity purchases by corporations, associations, and others. For details, contact the publisher at the following address:

Connect with Janay Price:

Instagram:
@janay_lcsw

Email:
janay.jpc@gmail.com

4711 Forest Drive Ste 3 #291
Columbia, SC 29206

ISBN: 978-0-578-90148-0

About the Author

Janay Price is a licensed clinical social worker with a bachelor's and master's degree in social work. Janay was attracted to the field of social work because she wanted to identify the problems of her community - locally and nationally; then offer solutions. If there are no solutions, Janay is eager to create them.

In 2013, Janay became a self-employed psychotherapist. Although she enjoyed being self-employed, she aspired to do more and give more, so in 2016 she decided to become a full-time entrepreneur. She knew very little about leading an organization; however, she knew that most successful businesses offer solutions to problems, which her background in social work equipped her to do.

With no capital, no connections, and her dream, she moved to a new state to start a mental health organization for the geriatric population. At the time of this publication, the company has been operating for 4 years and has provided psychotherapy and prescriptive treatment of psychotropic medication to well over 1,000 seniors in 13 cities throughout South Carolina.

Contact Premier Counseling, LLC at www.premiercounselingllc.org.

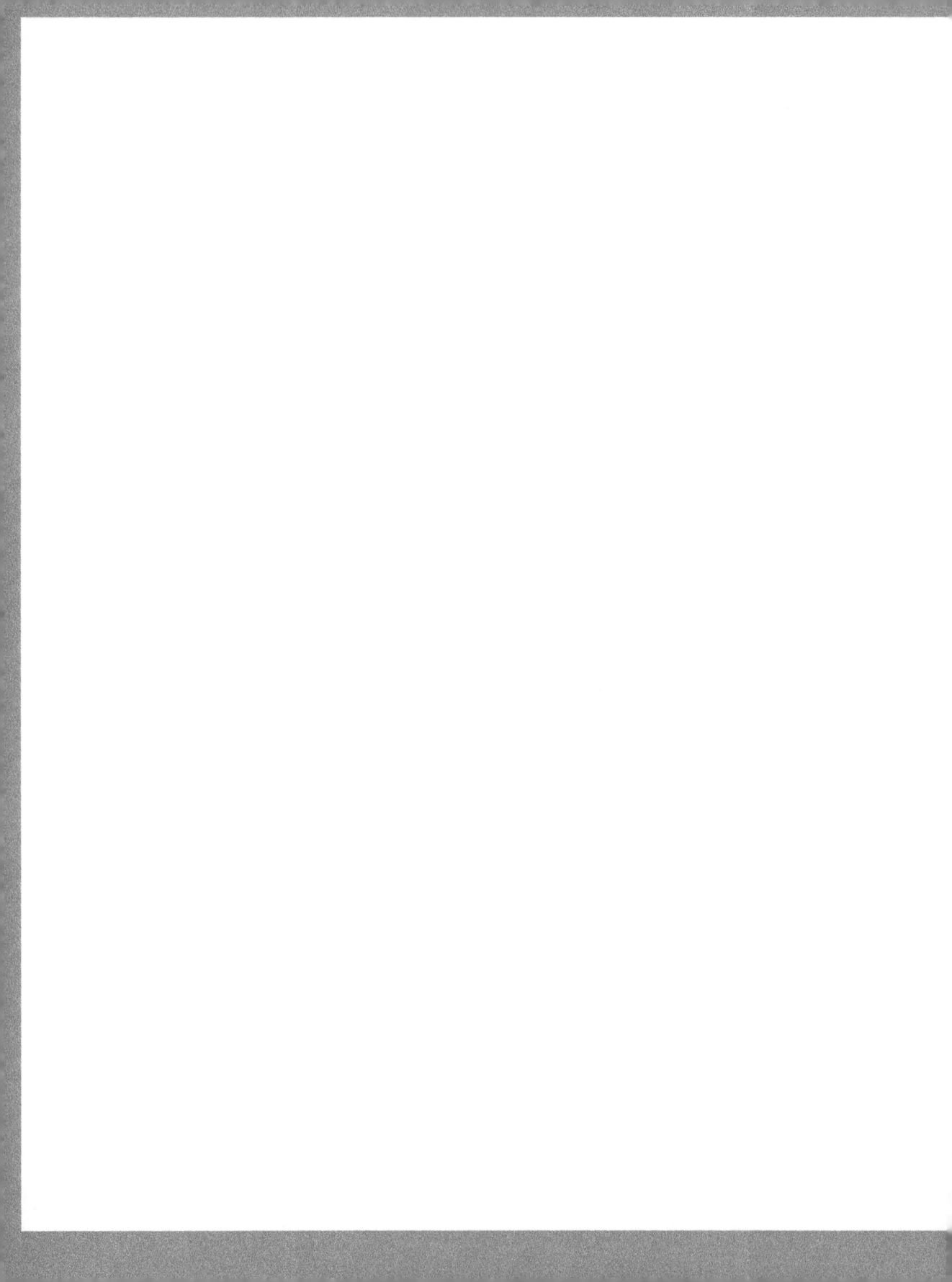

Dedication

This book is dedicated to my parents. Thank you for speaking encouraging words to me about my business and goals during the moments it was difficult for me to find the words for myself.

I also dedicate this book to new entrepreneurs passionate about their services and products, but who may feel discouraged and as if their dreams will never be their reality. I see you and I admire your zeal.

Benefits of Positive Affirmations

Positive affirmations serve to reprogram negative thoughts about yourself. If one can change the way she/he thinks, behaviors will change, which will lead to positive outcomes; ultimately creating the desired life.

How To Use This Workbook

This book will take you on a 100-day journey to becoming the entrepreneur you desire to be. For the next 100 days, commit to starting your day with a positive affirmation and reflect on how the affirmation will take you and your business to the next level.

You will find calendar pages in the back of the book to assist you in being intentional with your days. Use the calendar pages to schedule short-term goals, plan meetings, and track your progress. Writing your meetings, projects, goals, and deadlines in this journal will give you a snapshot of the progress you have made along the way.

Identifying Your "Why"

Identifying your "why" is necessary for every entrepreneur. Your "why" will motivate you to continue striving towards your goals on the challenging days of the entrepreneurial journey. Discovering your "why" is much more complex than people think. It requires answering a series of questions before truly knowing your "why." These questions will lead you to the heart of your personal mission and therefore the heart of your business.

What led you to create your product/service?

_____
_____
_____
_____
_____
_____
_____
_____
_____
_____
_____
_____
_____
_____
_____
_____

Why is your business unique?

_____

_____

_____

_____

_____

_____

_____

_____

_____

What is the purpose of your company?

_____

_____

_____

_____

_____

_____

_____

_____

_____

What problems will your business solve in your community or the world?

_____
_____
_____
_____
_____
_____
_____
_____
_____
_____

What are your personal and professional beliefs?

_____
_____
_____
_____
_____
_____
_____
_____
_____
_____

How will your business improve your life and the life of those you love?

_____
_____
_____
_____
_____
_____
_____
_____
_____
_____

Now that you have answered some of the hard questions, what is your "why"?

_____
_____
_____
_____
_____
_____
_____
_____
_____
_____

DAY 1

My Affirmation of the Day

"The business I desire to have also wants me."

What are your initial thoughts after saying this affirmation aloud? Have you ever thought about your business goals this way?

_____

_____

_____

_____

_____

_____

_____

_____

_____

_____

_____

_____

_____

Repeat the Affirmation of the Day.

DAY 2

My Affirmation of the Day

"I have the necessary skills to complete my daily tasks; if I am without the skill, I have the skills to find someone who has them."

List the areas where you feel strong and the areas where you feel limited. Think about the professionals around you that can help you with your limited areas; if you feel you cannot grow in that area, outsource to the professional who will excel in that area and take your business to the next level.

_____

_____

_____

_____

_____

_____

_____

_____

_____

_____

Repeat the Affirmation of the Day.

DAY 3

My Affirmation of the Day

"Today I will perform better than I did yesterday."

Thinking about the business owner you hope to be in the future can be intimidating. Simply focus on being great today. What will you do today to be the best version of yourself?

_____

_____

_____

_____

_____

_____

_____

_____

_____

_____

_____

_____

Repeat the Affirmation of the Day.

My Affirmation of the Day

"All my efforts and my thoughts
will lead me to the success
I am seeking."

The way we spend our time, as well as the things we allow to occupy our thoughts, will determine our future. Do your thoughts and actions support your goals?

_____

_____

_____

_____

_____

_____

_____

_____

_____

_____

_____

_____

_____

Repeat the Affirmation of the Day.

DAY 5

My Affirmation of the Day

"Every encounter is an opportunity."

Think about the last two professionals you met (in-person or virtually), or the past 2 events you attended. Did you take advantage of the opportunity to grow your business or brand? If so, how? If not, what will you do when the next opportunity occurs?

_____

_____

_____

_____

_____

_____

_____

_____

_____

_____

_____

_____

Repeat the Affirmation of the Day.

DAY 6

My Affirmation of the Day

"I can handle the challenges of today."

In business, challenges are inevitable. How will you conquer the challenges of today?

_____

_____

_____

_____

_____

_____

_____

_____

_____

_____

_____

_____

Repeat the Affirmation of the Day.

DAY 7

My Affirmation of the Day

"Today I choose happiness."

Happiness is a choice. We achieve happiness by focusing on the good parts of each day. Identify one thing in business that makes you happy today.

_____

_____

_____

_____

_____

_____

_____

_____

_____

_____

_____

_____

_____

Repeat the Affirmation of the Day.

My Affirmation of the Day

"The worries of tomorrow will not be on today's 'To Do List'."

Eighty-five percent of the things people worry about never happen. Focus on the needs and tasks of today and "worry" about tomorrow, tomorrow. Jot down today's tasks and the ways you plan to execute your list.

_____

_____

_____

_____

_____

_____

_____

_____

_____

_____

_____

_____

_____

Repeat the Affirmation of the Day.

DAY 9

My Affirmation of the Day

"I attract great opportunities."

Believe that great things are coming your way! Write down the opportunities that you are hoping for within the next thirty days.

_____

_____

_____

_____

_____

_____

_____

_____

_____

_____

_____

_____

Repeat the Affirmation of the Day.

DAY 10

My Affirmation of the Day

*"I can create the future
I hope for."*

You are in control, take charge of the future of your business. Where do you see your business in the next twelve months?

_____

_____

_____

_____

_____

_____

_____

_____

_____

_____

_____

_____

_____

Repeat the Affirmation of the Day.

10 Day Check-Up

How has your mindset shifted about your business in the past 10 days?

Write about the progress you have made in the past ten days. Remember, each day you work on your business goals is a day of progress. Also, identify what you want to accomplish in the upcoming ten days and the actions you will take to make these short-term goals your reality.

_____

_____

_____

_____

_____

_____

_____

_____

_____

_____

_____

_____

_____

_____

DAY 11

My Affirmation of the Day

"I am resilient, I will always bounce back."

You can expect to have bumps on the road during your entrepreneurial journey, but how do you plan to move past them?

_____

_____

_____

_____

_____

_____

_____

_____

_____

_____

_____

_____

_____

Repeat the Affirmation of the Day.

DAY 12

My Affirmation of the Day

"I am stronger than the challenges I face."

There is a saying, "You don't know how strong you are until you have to be strong." Reflect on a time in business when you made it through a difficult time.

_____

_____

_____

_____

_____

_____

_____

_____

_____

_____

_____

_____

_____

Repeat the Affirmation of the Day.

DAY 13

My Affirmation of the Day

"What I have to offer is enough."

You are enough! Highlight your talents, skills, and strengths today. Why do your consumers or community need your product/service?

_____

_____

_____

_____

_____

_____

_____

_____

_____

_____

_____

_____

Repeat the Affirmation of the Day.

DAY 14

My Affirmation of the Day

*"I have a history of
recovering from every obstacle
on my path."*

The fact that you are still striving towards your goals is proof that you have what it takes. Write about one challenge you overcame that you are proud of.

_____

_____

_____

_____

_____

_____

_____

_____

_____

_____

_____

_____

_____

Repeat the Affirmation of the Day.

DAY 15

My Affirmation of the Day

"I let go of my negative thoughts about money and I welcome wealth into my life."

When you do great work, money will follow. How will you build a healthy relationship with money as your company's revenue increases?

_____

_____

_____

_____

_____

_____

_____

_____

_____

_____

_____

_____

Repeat the Affirmation of the Day.

DAY 16

My Affirmation of the Day

*"I can change my mind and
I will not feel guilty about it."*

The needs of your company will be ever-changing. There may be times when you must change your plans. That is okay! Are there things you need to adjust but are hesitant to do so?

_____

_____

_____

_____

_____

_____

_____

_____

_____

_____

_____

_____

Repeat the Affirmation of the Day.

DAY 17

My Affirmation of the Day

"I will not quit."

What will happen if you quit? Write about the consequences of that decision.

_____

_____

_____

_____

_____

_____

_____

_____

_____

_____

_____

_____

_____

Repeat the Affirmation of the Day.

My Affirmation of the Day

"I will not feel guilty about pursuing my dreams."

Guilt should only be present when one has done something illegal or immoral; pursuing your dreams should not make you feel guilty. Dissect your feelings of guilt and write down the reasons why your goals of entrepreneurship are necessary.

_____

_____

_____

_____

_____

_____

_____

_____

_____

_____

_____

_____

Repeat the Affirmation of the Day.

DAY 19

My Affirmation of the Day

"I am a great leader."

List three reasons why you are a great leader.

_____

_____

_____

_____

_____

_____

_____

_____

_____

_____

_____

_____

_____

_____

Repeat the Affirmation of the Day.

My Affirmation of the Day

"My goal is to go far, not fast."

Rushing through and creating shortcuts rarely pays off. What steps have you tried to skip in this process? How will skipping these steps hurt you in the future?

_____

_____

_____

_____

_____

_____

_____

_____

_____

_____

_____

_____

_____

Repeat the Affirmation of the Day.

10 Day Check-Up

How has your mindset shifted about your business in the past 10 days?

Write about the progress you have made in the past ten days. Remember each day you work on your business goals is a day of progress. Also, identify what you want to accomplish in the upcoming ten days and the actions you will take to make these short-term goals your reality.

_____

_____

_____

_____

_____

_____

_____

_____

_____

_____

_____

_____

_____

_____

_____

_____

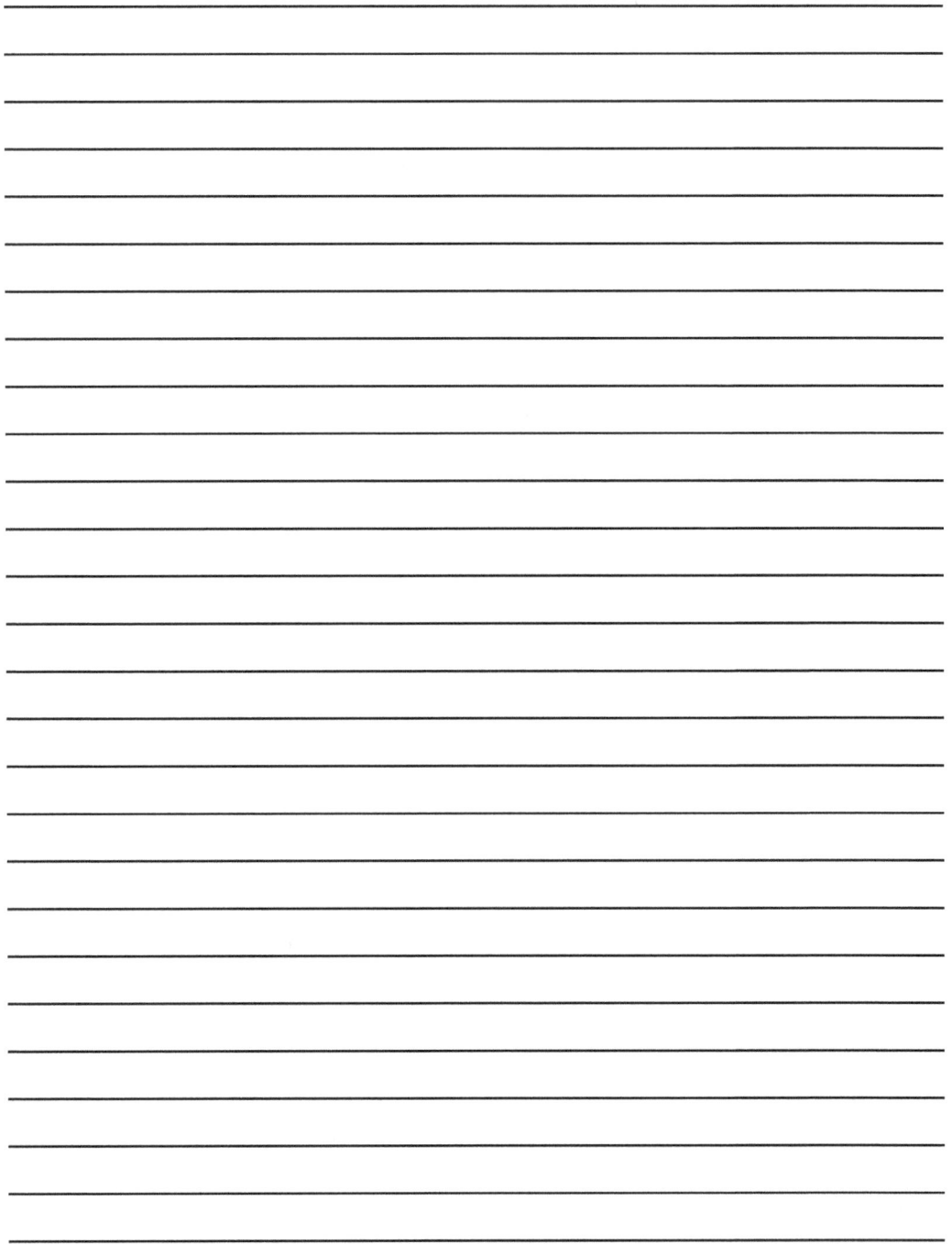

DAY 21

My Affirmation of the Day

*"My business journey is
mine; I do not have to
compare it to others."*

Thanks to the media, we are inundated with images of success and what it should look like. Have you been comparing your journey to others'? If so, why? Are the comparisons overwhelming? Write your thoughts.

_____

_____

_____

_____

_____

_____

_____

_____

_____

_____

_____

_____

Repeat the Affirmation of the Day.

My Affirmation of the Day

*"My best may not be perfect,
but it is enough."*

Have you been procrastinating on tasks because of fear that the execution will not be perfect? Why do you feel things have to be perfect? Write reasons why your best is enough.

_____

_____

_____

_____

_____

_____

_____

_____

_____

_____

_____

Repeat the Affirmation of the Day.

My Affirmation of the Day

"Today, I am grateful."

List five things you are grateful for in business.

_____

_____

_____

_____

_____

_____

_____

_____

_____

_____

_____

_____

_____

_____

Repeat the Affirmation of the Day.

DAY 24

My Affirmation of the Day

"My product/service will impact the lives of others in a positive way."

Why do your consumers or your community need your product/service?

_____

_____

_____

_____

_____

_____

_____

_____

_____

_____

_____

_____

Repeat the Affirmation of the Day.

My Affirmation of the Day

"I am blessed."

List three reasons why you feel blessed and how you will use your blessings to take your business to the next level.

_____

_____

_____

_____

_____

_____

_____

_____

_____

_____

_____

_____

_____

Repeat the Affirmation of the Day.

My Affirmation of the Day

"I have the capacity to effectively lead my team."

What leadership characteristics do you have? How will you use them to grow your business?

_____

_____

_____

_____

_____

_____

_____

_____

_____

_____

_____

_____

Repeat the Affirmation of the Day.

My Affirmation of the Day

"I am an expert in my industry."

Review your resume or CV. Acknowledge and celebrate your industry wins. If you are new to this industry, highlight your passion and knowledge surrounding your product/service.

_____

_____

_____

_____

_____

_____

_____

_____

_____

_____

_____

_____

_____

Repeat the Affirmation of the Day.

DAY 28

My Affirmation of the Day

"I do not have to choose between family, friends, and my business. I can find balance."

There is a way to have it all. There are 168 hours in a week, be intentional with every hour. Write down how you currently spend your 168 hours; if you are not pleased with the way you are spending your time, adjust it to include the social, professional, personal, and spiritual connections that you desire. The time may not be evenly distributed, but there is a way to create time for each area of your life.

_____

_____

_____

_____

_____

_____

_____

_____

_____

_____

_____

_____

Repeat the Affirmation of the Day.

DAY 29

My Affirmation of the Day

"Everything is aligning in my favor."

Opportunities and missed opportunities are all to your advantage. Reflect on a time during this journey where a missed opportunity was a good thing.

_____

_____

_____

_____

_____

_____

_____

_____

_____

_____

_____

_____

_____

Repeat the Affirmation of the Day.

DAY 30

My Affirmation of the Day

"I am proud of myself."

Celebrate yourself today. List five reasons why you are proud of yourself and your business.

_____

_____

_____

_____

_____

_____

_____

_____

_____

_____

_____

_____

_____

_____

Repeat the Affirmation of the Day.

10 Day Check-Up

How has your mindset shifted about your business in the past 10 days?

Write about the progress you have made in the past ten days. Remember each day you work on your business goals is a day of progress. Also, identify what you want to accomplish in the upcoming ten days and the actions you will take to make these short-term goals your reality.

_____

_____

_____

_____

_____

_____

_____

_____

_____

_____

_____

_____

_____

_____

DAY 31

My Affirmation of the Day

*"It may not happen now, but
it will happen."*

As you are waiting for a large order, contract, or engagement; how are you spending your time? How can you actively wait?

_____

_____

_____

_____

_____

_____

_____

_____

_____

_____

_____

_____

Repeat the Affirmation of the Day.

DAY 32

My Affirmation of the Day

"I am excited about my future."

What is in store for you? Write it out. Dream big!

_____

_____

_____

_____

_____

_____

_____

_____

_____

_____

_____

_____

_____

Repeat the Affirmation of the Day.

DAY 33

My Affirmation of the Day

"I am going to make it; I will succeed!"

You must believe that the success you are striving for is attainable. Why are your goals realistic?

_____

_____

_____

_____

_____

_____

_____

_____

_____

_____

_____

_____

_____

Repeat the Affirmation of the Day.

My Affirmation of the Day

"I make the conscious decision to keep going because I have what it takes."

List the traits you possess that make you a great business owner.

_____

_____

_____

_____

_____

_____

_____

_____

_____

_____

_____

_____

_____

Repeat the Affirmation of the Day.

DAY 35

My Affirmation of the Day

"I am not greedy. My charges and fees reflect my value."

What are you worth? What value do you and your product/service add to your consumers and community?

_____

_____

_____

_____

_____

_____

_____

_____

_____

_____

_____

_____

_____

Repeat the Affirmation of the Day.

My Affirmation of the Day

"I survived hundreds of bad days. I will get through today."

One way to survive a bad day is to make progress. No matter how small, what can you do today to get you one step closer to your goal?

_____

_____

_____

_____

_____

_____

_____

_____

_____

_____

_____

_____

Repeat the Affirmation of the Day.

DAY 37

My Affirmation of the Day

*"I am thankful for a new
day to learn new things."*

What will you learn today? Read an article, research your target population, connect with another expert in your industry; then write down one thing you learned and how you will apply it to your business.

_____

_____

_____

_____

_____

_____

_____

_____

_____

_____

_____

Repeat the Affirmation of the Day.

DAY 38

My Affirmation of the Day

"The world needs what I have."

If you do not sell your product or offer your service, how will it negatively affect your consumers?

_____

_____

_____

_____

_____

_____

_____

_____

_____

_____

_____

_____

Repeat the Affirmation of the Day.

DAY 39

My Affirmation of the Day

"Everything moves the needle."

It is easy to feel like your efforts are not paying off. Reflect on the small things you have done or will do that can change the trajectory of your business.

_____

_____

_____

_____

_____

_____

_____

_____

_____

_____

_____

_____

_____

Repeat the Affirmation of the Day.

DAY 40

My Affirmation of the Day

"Financial freedom is in my future."

Once you reach your financial goals how will you feel? What will you do because of the freedom?

_____

_____

_____

_____

_____

_____

_____

_____

_____

_____

_____

_____

Repeat the Affirmation of the Day.

10 Day Check-Up

How has your mindset shifted about your business in the past 10 days?

Write about the progress you have made in the past ten days. Remember each day you work on your business goals is a day of progress. Also, identify what you want to accomplish in the upcoming ten days and the actions you will take to make these short-term goals your reality.

_____

_____

_____

_____

_____

_____

_____

_____

_____

_____

_____

_____

_____

_____

_____

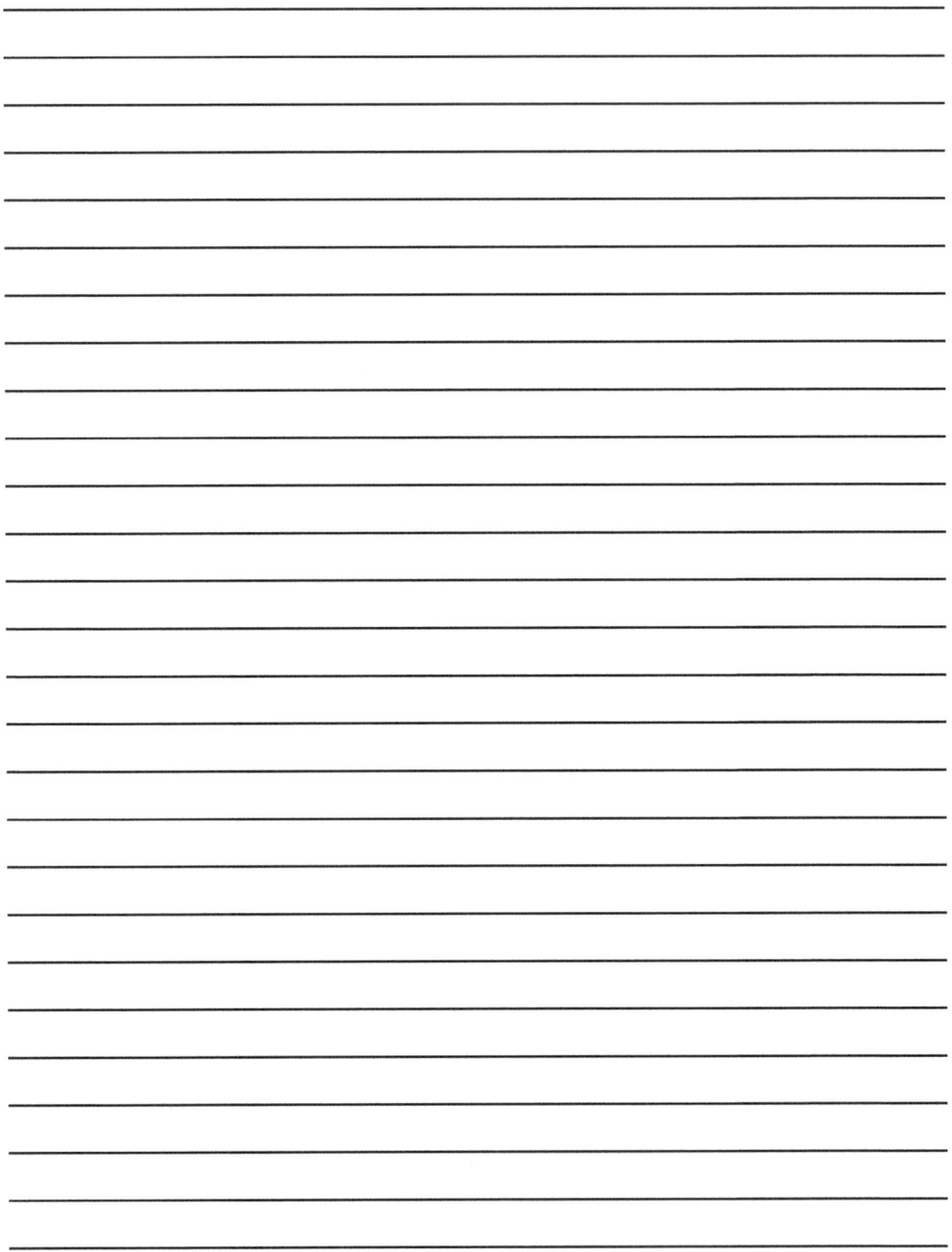

DAY 41

My Affirmation of the Day

"I will focus on my work instead of the rewards - the rewards will come because of my great work."

Which have you been focusing more on lately, the work or the rewards?

_____

_____

_____

_____

_____

_____

_____

_____

_____

_____

_____

_____

_____

Repeat the Affirmation of the Day.

DAY 42

My Affirmation of the Day

"Whenever I complete the task will be the perfect time."

It is easy to feel like you are behind schedule or that you should be much further in your entrepreneurial journey. Extend yourself grace today; your pace is perfect. How will you extend yourself grace today?

_____

_____

_____

_____

_____

_____

_____

_____

_____

_____

Repeat the Affirmation of the Day.

DAY 43

My Affirmation of the Day

"I will let go of things I cannot control."

Obstacles are inevitable in business. What obstacles are you currently facing? Of those obstacles which ones are out of your control?

_____

_____

_____

_____

_____

_____

_____

_____

_____

_____

_____

_____

_____

Repeat the Affirmation of the Day.

DAY 44

My Affirmation of the Day

"Negative thoughts will not control my day. I am focusing on the good."

List two great things that have happened today.

_____

_____

_____

_____

_____

_____

_____

_____

_____

_____

_____

_____

_____

_____

Repeat the Affirmation of the Day.

DAY 45

My Affirmation of the Day

"I believe in my ability to succeed."

Why do you believe you will succeed?

_____

_____

_____

_____

_____

_____

_____

_____

_____

_____

_____

_____

_____

Repeat the Affirmation of the Day.

DAY 46

My Affirmation of the Day

"I am on the right track."

List three reasons why you know you are on the path to success.

_____

_____

_____

_____

_____

_____

_____

_____

_____

_____

_____

_____

Repeat the Affirmation of the Day.

My Affirmation of the Day

"I am in the right place at the right time."

Why is your service or product necessary now?

_____

_____

_____

_____

_____

_____

_____

_____

_____

_____

_____

_____

Repeat the Affirmation of the Day.

DAY 48

My Affirmation of the Day

"This journey will come with challenges; I will face them with a positive attitude."

Write two positive affirmations you can say when challenges arise.

_____

_____

_____

_____

_____

_____

_____

_____

_____

_____

_____

_____

_____

Repeat the Affirmation of the Day.

DAY 49

My Affirmation of the Day

"My business is successful."

Document your business accomplishments thus far. No accomplishment is too small.

_____

_____

_____

_____

_____

_____

_____

_____

_____

_____

_____

_____

Repeat the Affirmation of the Day.

My Affirmation of the Day

"Several people believe in my vision and are willing to help me. I can also add value to them as professionals."

You may feel like you are on this journey alone, but your peers are willing to lend a helping hand when needed. List two people and ways they can help you; then write the value you will provide them.

_____

_____

_____

_____

_____

_____

_____

_____

_____

Repeat the Affirmation of the Day.

10 Day Check-Up

*How has your mindset shifted
about your business in the past
10 days?*

Write about the progress you have made in the past ten days. Remember each day you work on your business goals is a day of progress. Also, identify what you want to accomplish in the upcoming ten days and the actions you will take to make these short-term goals your reality.

_____

_____

_____

_____

_____

_____

_____

_____

_____

_____

_____

_____

_____

_____

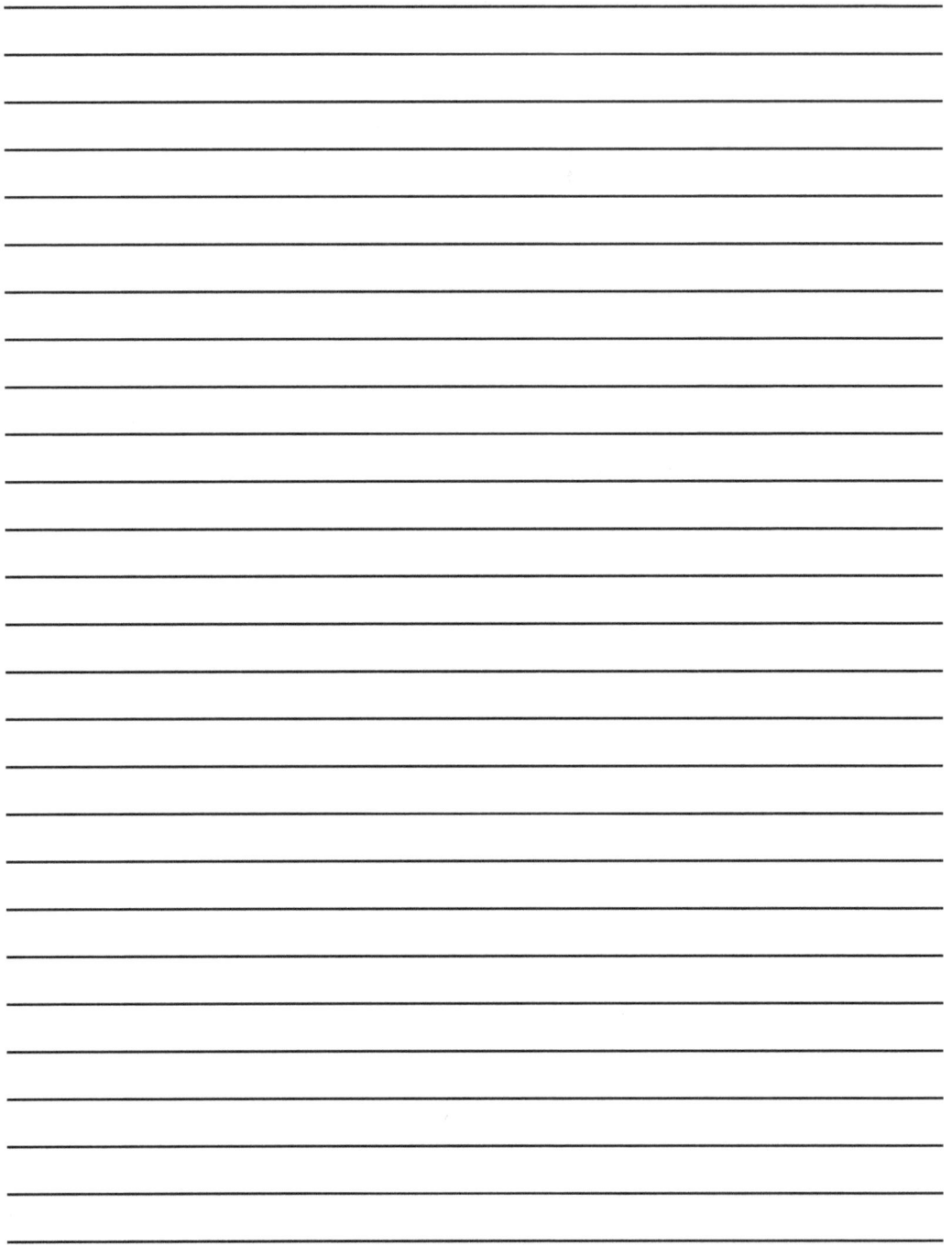

DAY 51

My Affirmation of the Day

"I am one step closer to my professional goals."

Take five minutes to reflect on your progress. What did you discover? Look how far you've come!

_____

_____

_____

_____

_____

_____

_____

_____

_____

_____

_____

_____

Repeat the Affirmation of the Day.

My Affirmation of the Day

"I am devoted to my purpose."

To be devoted is to be loyal and extremely loving. Reflect on your devotion to your purpose.

_____

_____

_____

_____

_____

_____

_____

_____

_____

_____

_____

_____

Repeat the Affirmation of the Day.

My Affirmation of the Day

*"I do not have to figure it
all out at once."*

The hardest part is getting started. What can you get started on today even if you do not have it all figured out?

_____

_____

_____

_____

_____

_____

_____

_____

_____

_____

_____

_____

Repeat the Affirmation of the Day.

My Affirmation of the Day

"Every day that I work towards my company's vision is a great day of work."

What will be great about today's day of work?

_____

_____

_____

_____

_____

_____

_____

_____

_____

_____

_____

_____

Repeat the Affirmation of the Day.

DAY 55

My Affirmation of the Day

"I expect great things."

List three things that you expect to happen in the next 90 days for your business.

_____

_____

_____

_____

_____

_____

_____

_____

_____

_____

_____

_____

_____

Repeat the Affirmation of the Day.

DAY 56

My Affirmation of the Day

"I am excited about the future of my business."

Where is your business going next? Write your 30-day, one-year, and five-year goals.

_____

_____

_____

_____

_____

_____

_____

_____

_____

_____

_____

_____

_____

Repeat the Affirmation of the Day.

DAY 57

My Affirmation of the Day

"I am on a powerful mission."

Write your company's mission statement. Read it aloud. Reflect.

_____

_____

_____

_____

_____

_____

_____

_____

_____

_____

_____

_____

Repeat the Affirmation of the Day.

DAY 58

My Affirmation of the Day

*"My goals are attainable;
they are not too big."*

Achieving a goal is simply completing several small tasks until you get the desired outcome. How can you break your goals down into smaller tasks?

_____

_____

_____

_____

_____

_____

_____

_____

_____

_____

_____

_____

_____

_____

Repeat the Affirmation of the Day.

DAY 59

My Affirmation of the Day

"Success is plentiful, there is more than enough for me."

It is not uncommon to feel like your service or product will not be received by your consumers because of competitors in the industry. Know that there is enough space for you to occupy and flourish. Reflect on this statement.

_____

_____

_____

_____

_____

_____

_____

_____

_____

_____

_____

_____

Repeat the Affirmation of the Day.

My Affirmation of the Day

*"My professional dreams
will soon be my reality."*

Visualize yourself in a place where your ultimate business goal has been met. What will this moment feel like for you?

_____

_____

_____

_____

_____

_____

_____

_____

_____

_____

_____

_____

_____

Repeat the Affirmation of the Day.

10 Day Check-Up

How has your mindset shifted about your business in the past 10 days?

Write about the progress you have made in the past ten days. Remember each day you work on your business goals is a day of progress. Also, identify what you want to accomplish in the upcoming ten days and the actions you will take to make these short-term goals your reality.

_____

_____

_____

_____

_____

_____

_____

_____

_____

_____

_____

_____

_____

_____

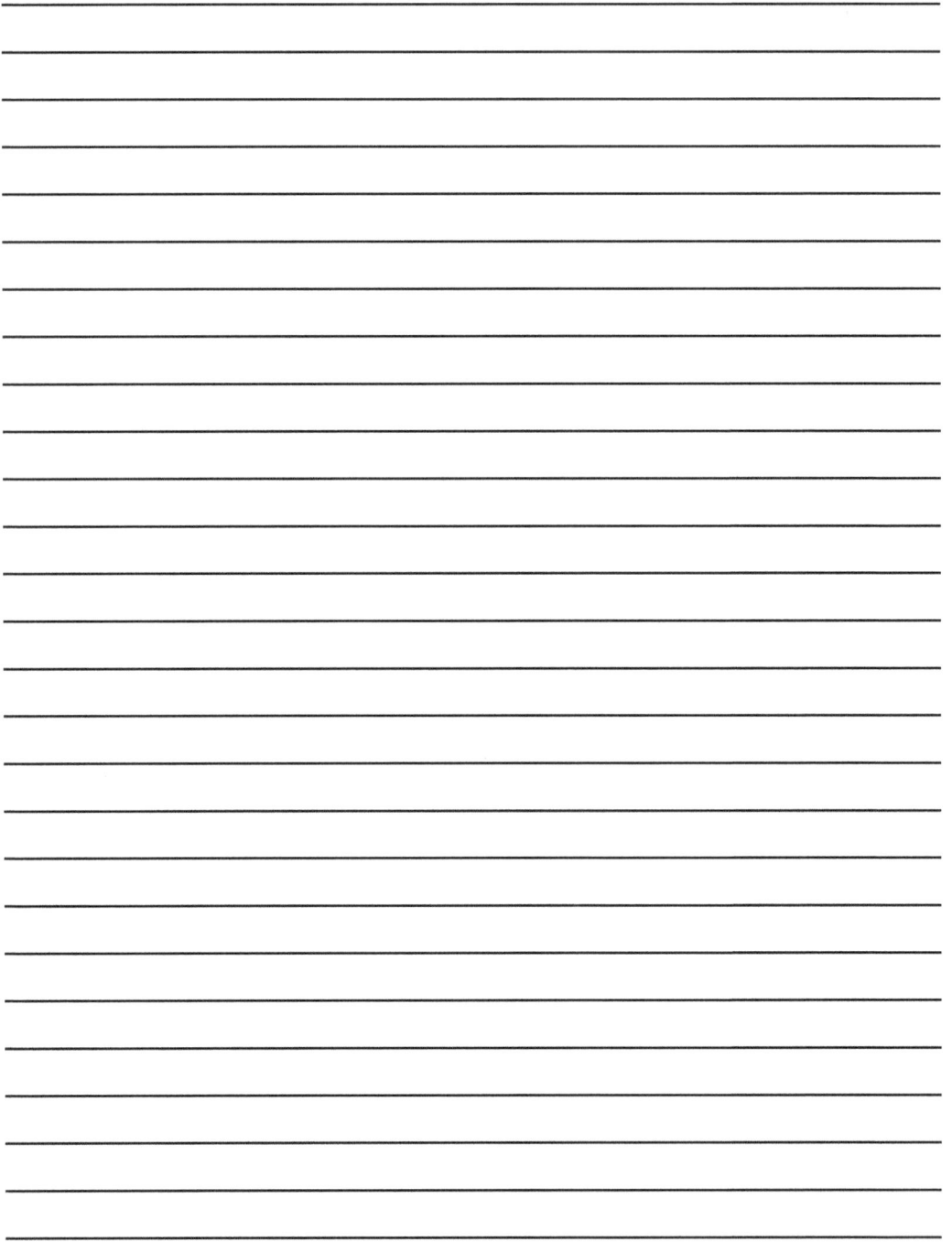

DAY 61

My Affirmation of the Day

"Feeling defeated and being defeated are not the same. I can and will press forward."

If you have feelings of defeat today, process those feelings and create a plan to overcome them. You will overcome!

_____

_____

_____

_____

_____

_____

_____

_____

_____

_____

_____

_____

Repeat the Affirmation of the Day.

DAY 62

My Affirmation of the Day

"I cannot change my past decisions and I am okay with that."

Give yourself permission to forgive yourself for your past decisions. You have learned from them and they are necessary experiences to take you to the next level. How can you use the outcome of those decisions to take your company to the next level?

_____

_____

_____

_____

_____

_____

_____

_____

_____

_____

_____

Repeat the Affirmation of the Day.

My Affirmation of the Day

"My business is a blessing, not a burden."

It is easy to become overwhelmed by the responsibilities that come with being an entrepreneur. Simply saying "I get to do _____;" as opposed to saying, "I have to do _____." Will change the outcome of your day.

For example: "I get to wake up each morning and work diligently towards the goals of my business;" as opposed to, "I have to wake up early to start on this never-ending to-do list." Replace two of your "I have to" statements with two "I get to" statements.

_____

_____

_____

_____

_____

_____

_____

_____

_____

Repeat the Affirmation of the Day.

DAY 64

My Affirmation of the Day

"Today will be the day that my efforts change lives."

What will you do today to make your consumers' lives better?

_____

_____

_____

_____

_____

_____

_____

_____

_____

_____

_____

_____

Repeat the Affirmation of the Day.

DAY 65

My Affirmation of the Day

"I have the power to control my thoughts about my business today."

Take charge today, what will you choose to focus on?

_____

_____

_____

_____

_____

_____

_____

_____

_____

_____

_____

_____

_____

Repeat the Affirmation of the Day.

My Affirmation of the Day

*"I love the responsibilities
I have as a business owner."*

What do you love most about being an entrepreneur?

_____

_____

_____

_____

_____

_____

_____

_____

_____

_____

_____

_____

Repeat the Affirmation of the Day.

My Affirmation of the Day

"I am the expert of my business."

Taking advice from colleagues, family, and friends is not a bad thing, but be mindful that you do not allow others to change the vision for your company. Have you been negatively influenced by the advice of others?

_____

_____

_____

_____

_____

_____

_____

_____

_____

_____

_____

_____

Repeat the Affirmation of the Day.

My Affirmation of the Day

"I deserve to lead my company; I have earned this position."

Imposter Syndrome is when someone feels like a fraud or she/he doubts their abilities. It typically affects high achievers. Are you questioning your abilities? If so, why? You deserve to be here!

_____

_____

_____

_____

_____

_____

_____

_____

_____

_____

_____

_____

Repeat the Affirmation of the Day.

DAY 69

My Affirmation of the Day

"My hard work is paying off."

How do you know your hard work is paying off?

_____

_____

_____

_____

_____

_____

_____

_____

_____

_____

_____

_____

Repeat the Affirmation of the Day.

My Affirmation of the Day

"My goals are not far-fetched."

List three reasons why this affirmation is true.

_____

_____

_____

_____

_____

_____

_____

_____

_____

_____

_____

_____

_____

Repeat the Affirmation of the Day.

10 Day Check-Up

How has your mindset shifted about your business in the past 10 days?

Write about the progress you have made in the past ten days. Remember each day you work on your business goals is a day of progress. Also, identify what you want to accomplish in the upcoming ten days and the actions you will take to make these short-term goals your reality.

_____

_____

_____

_____

_____

_____

_____

_____

_____

_____

_____

_____

_____

_____

_____

_____

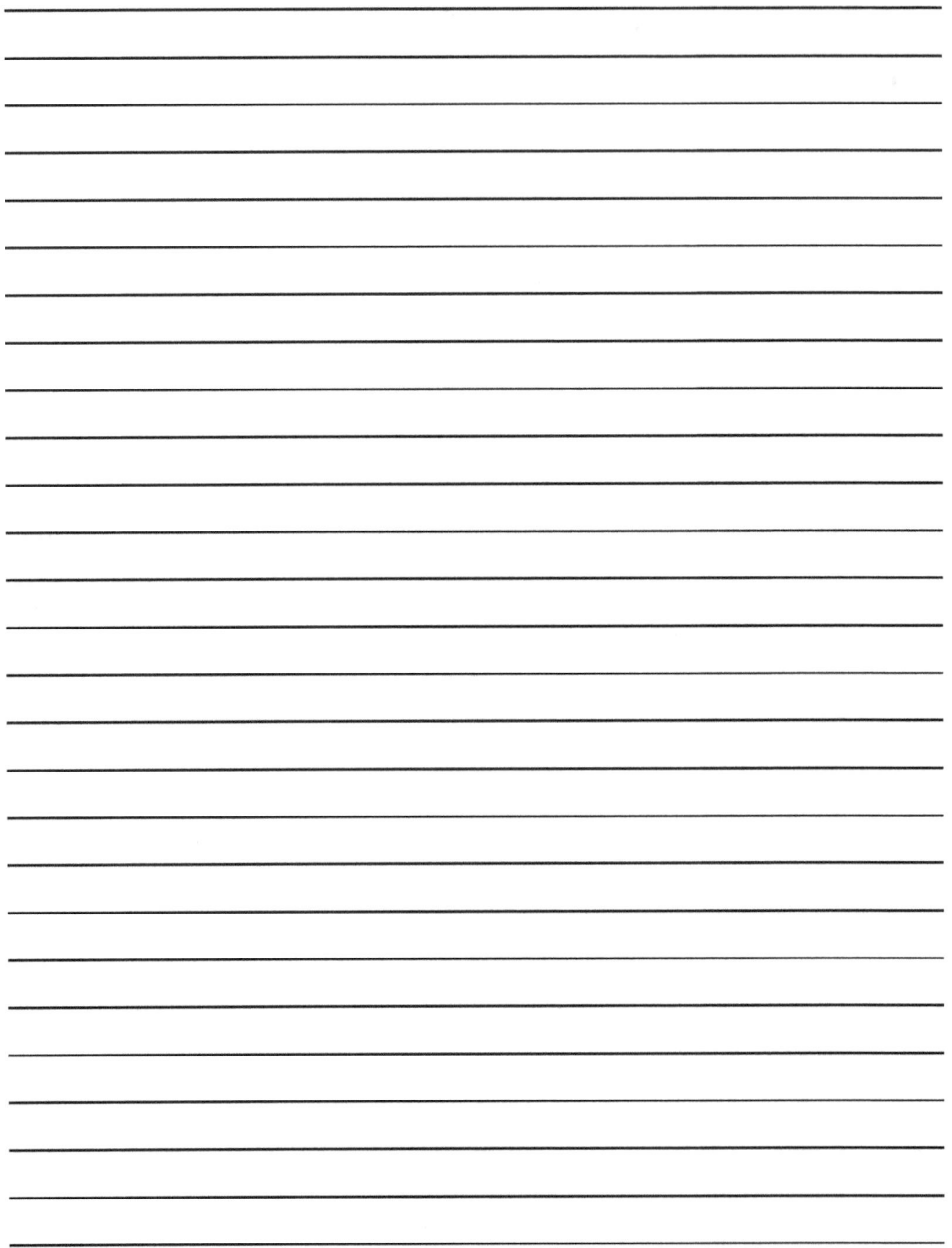

DAY 71

My Affirmation of the Day

"My fears will not hinder me from achieving my goals."

What will you do to overcome your fears?

_____

_____

_____

_____

_____

_____

_____

_____

_____

_____

_____

_____

_____

Repeat the Affirmation of the Day.

DAY 72

My Affirmation of the Day

"I am thankful."

List ten things you are thankful for.

_____

_____

_____

_____

_____

_____

_____

_____

_____

_____

_____

_____

Repeat the Affirmation of the Day.

DAY 73

My Affirmation of the Day

"I will not minimize my success; I am proud of myself."

What are you most proud of?

_____

_____

_____

_____

_____

_____

_____

_____

_____

_____

_____

_____

Repeat the Affirmation of the Day.

DAY 74

My Affirmation of the Day

*"I have gone far, and I can
go further."*

It is time for a recap. What have you accomplished in business over the last 70 days?

_____

_____

_____

_____

_____

_____

_____

_____

_____

_____

_____

_____

Repeat the Affirmation of the Day.

My Affirmation of the Day

"The vision I have for my company is clear, I will not allow people or things to blur it."

Write your company's vision statement. Read it aloud.

_____

_____

_____

_____

_____

_____

_____

_____

_____

_____

_____

_____

Repeat the Affirmation of the Day.

My Affirmation of the Day

"The impact I have on my community and in the lives of my consumers through my business will be mind-blowing."

Write down the impact you will make. Think big!

_____

_____

_____

_____

_____

_____

_____

_____

_____

_____

_____

_____

Repeat the Affirmation of the Day.

DAY 77

My Affirmation of the Day

"I am capable; my fears and frustrations will not hinder me."

What is your greatest strength? How will you use it to grow your business?

_____

_____

_____

_____

_____

_____

_____

_____

_____

_____

_____

_____

Repeat the Affirmation of the Day.

My Affirmation of the Day

"I have no doubt that my company will have continued success."

Why do you believe in your company's success?

_____

_____

_____

_____

_____

_____

_____

_____

_____

_____

_____

_____

_____

Repeat the Affirmation of the Day.

My Affirmation of the Day

"I am in control of my destiny."

What can you control today?

_____

_____

_____

_____

_____

_____

_____

_____

_____

_____

_____

_____

_____

Repeat the Affirmation of the Day.

DAY 80

My Affirmation of the Day

"Stepping outside of my comfort zone is exciting."

What could you do if you were not nervous or afraid of being uncomfortable?

_____

_____

_____

_____

_____

_____

_____

_____

_____

_____

_____

_____

Repeat the Affirmation of the Day.

10 Day Check-Up

*How has your mindset
shifted about your business in
the past 10 days?*

Write about the progress you have made in the past ten days. Remember each day you work on your business goals is a day of progress. Also, identify what you want to accomplish in the upcoming ten days and the actions you will take to make these short-term goals your reality.

_____

_____

_____

_____

_____

_____

_____

_____

_____

_____

_____

_____

_____

_____

DAY 81

My Affirmation of the Day

"I cannot help everyone, and I am okay with that. The people I am meant to help will be helped."

Who is your ideal consumer? Why did you choose to target this population? Are you willing to say no to consumers who do not fit your target population? What are the benefits of focusing solely on your ideal consumer?

_____

_____

_____

_____

_____

_____

_____

_____

_____

_____

_____

Repeat the Affirmation of the Day.

My Affirmation of the Day

"I am proud of myself now; I do not have to wait until the goal is achieved to be proud."

What are you most proud of at this moment?

_____

_____

_____

_____

_____

_____

_____

_____

_____

_____

_____

_____

Repeat the Affirmation of the Day.

DAY 83

My Affirmation of the Day

*"I am mastering my ability
to persevere."*

How does this affirmation apply to you?

_____

_____

_____

_____

_____

_____

_____

_____

_____

_____

_____

_____

Repeat the Affirmation of the Day.

DAY 84

My Affirmation of the Day

"I am not greedy for wanting financial freedom."

What will you do for yourself and others once you gain financial freedom?

_____

_____

_____

_____

_____

_____

_____

_____

_____

_____

_____

_____

_____

Repeat the Affirmation of the Day.

DAY 85

My Affirmation of the Day

*"I will finish regardless of
how long it takes."*

Reflect on the way you feel when you do not reach your deadlines. Make a commitment to yourself that when these feelings arise you will keep going.

_____

_____

_____

_____

_____

_____

_____

_____

_____

_____

_____

_____

_____

Repeat the Affirmation of the Day.

My Affirmation of the Day

*"My hard work is paying off
and my dreams are coming
true."*

Write about your greatest accomplishment in the past seven days. No accomplishment is a small one. Remember, everything moves the needle!

_____
_____
_____
_____
_____
_____
_____
_____
_____
_____
_____
_____
_____

Repeat the Affirmation of the Day.

DAY 87

My Affirmation of the Day

"Things are working out for me."

Why do you believe that things are working out for you? What are the signs of this?

_____

_____

_____

_____

_____

_____

_____

_____

_____

_____

_____

_____

_____

Repeat the Affirmation of the Day.

DAY 88

My Affirmation of the Day

"My attitude determines good and bad days. Today will be a good day of business because I said so."

What will you accomplish today?

_____

_____

_____

_____

_____

_____

_____

_____

_____

_____

_____

_____

Repeat the Affirmation of the Day.

My Affirmation of the Day

"I do not have all the answers; that is okay. I will keep going anyway."

When you do not have the answers for the challenges in front of you, where can you find the solutions as you continue to move forward?

_____

_____

_____

_____

_____

_____

_____

_____

_____

_____

_____

_____

Repeat the Affirmation of the Day.

My Affirmation of the Day

"I am attracting wealth."

In what ways are you attracting wealth?

_____

_____

_____

_____

_____

_____

_____

_____

_____

_____

_____

_____

Repeat the Affirmation of the Day.

10 Day Check-Up

How has your mindset shifted about your business in the past 10 days?

Write about the progress you have made in the past ten days. Remember each day you work on your business goals is a day of progress. Also, identify what you want to accomplish in the upcoming ten days and the actions you will take to make these short-term goals your reality.

_____

_____

_____

_____

_____

_____

_____

_____

_____

_____

_____

_____

_____

_____

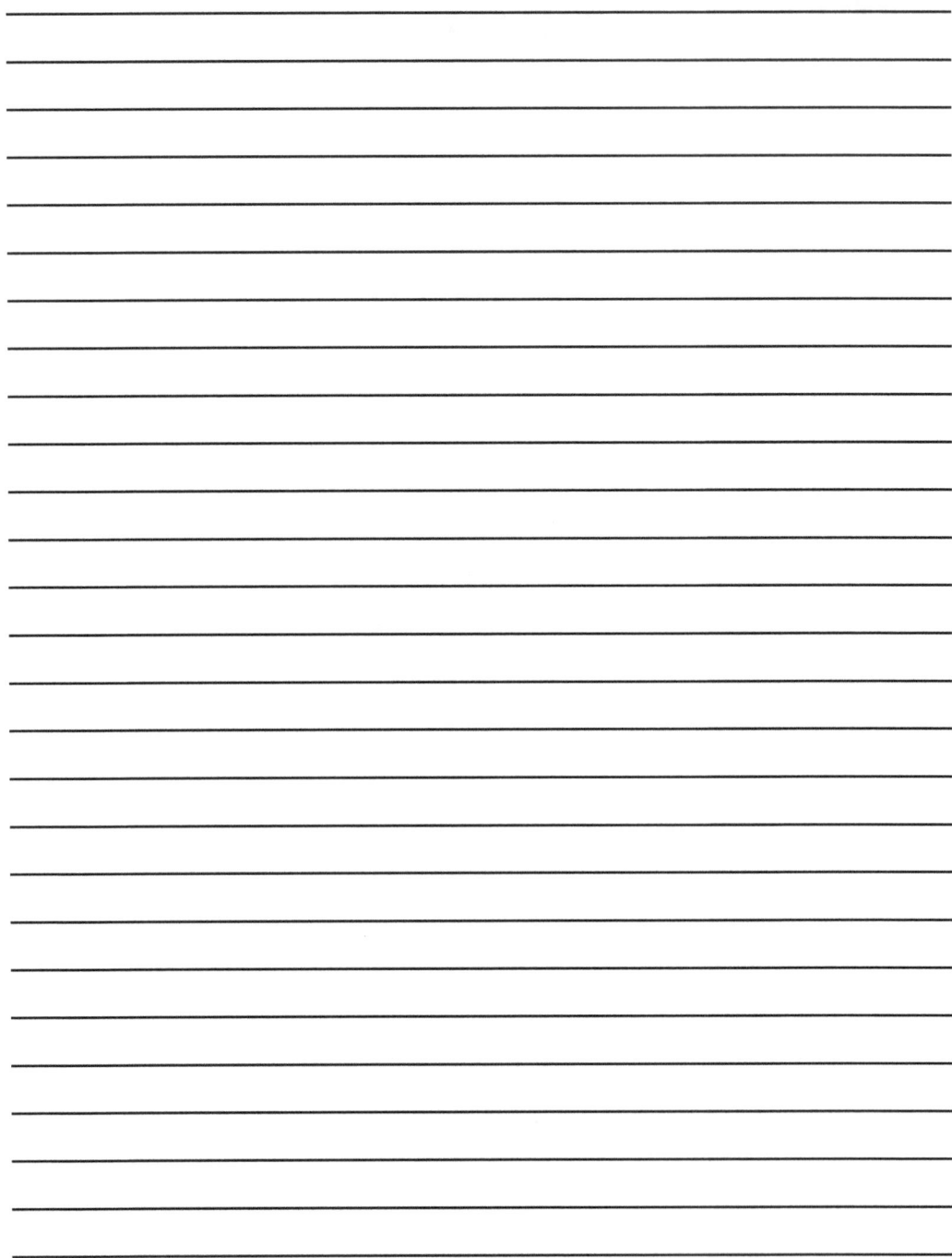

My Affirmation of the Day

"Each day I am becoming a better professional."

If you do not belong to a community of entrepreneurs, research groups in your area to connect with. If no groups are available, search social media. Being connected to like-minded individuals will help you become a better entrepreneur. List at least two entrepreneur groups.

_____

_____

_____

_____

_____

_____

_____

_____

_____

_____

_____

Repeat the Affirmation of the Day.

My Affirmation of the Day

"I will make the best decision for my brand — without feelings of guilt - even if others disagree."

Guilt is an emotion reserved for times when a person has done something illegal or immoral. List the things you have felt guilty about in your business and free yourself of the negative feelings.

_____

_____

_____

_____

_____

_____

_____

_____

_____

_____

_____

_____

Repeat the Affirmation of the Day.

My Affirmation of the Day

"Abundance is coming! I deserve it!"

List ten things you know you deserve. Follow this prompt for each, "I deserve_____."

_____

_____

_____

_____

_____

_____

_____

_____

_____

_____

_____

_____

Repeat the Affirmation of the Day.

DAY 94

My Affirmation of the Day

"I am neither weak nor lazy because I take breaks. I am taking care of myself and my company."

List three activities of self-care then add them to your calendar. Be intentional about taking breaks.

_____

_____

_____

_____

_____

_____

_____

_____

_____

_____

_____

_____

Repeat the Affirmation of the Day.

DAY 95

My Affirmation of the Day

*"Each day I am one day
closer to my dream."*

Track your progress. What have you done in the past 30 days that has moved you closer to your end goal?

_____

_____

_____

_____

_____

_____

_____

_____

_____

_____

_____

_____

Repeat the Affirmation of the Day.

My Affirmation of the Day

"I have people cheering for my company's success even when I feel alone."

List three people you can depend on and why.

_____

_____

_____

_____

_____

_____

_____

_____

_____

_____

_____

_____

_____

Repeat the Affirmation of the Day.

My Affirmation of the Day

*"I am open to new ideas
and new experiences."*

Identify two areas where you want to grow as an entrepreneur. Research a training either in-person or virtually that will contribute to your growth in the listed areas.

_____

_____

_____

_____

_____

_____

_____

_____

_____

_____

_____

_____

Repeat the Affirmation of the Day.

My Affirmation of the Day

"Pivoting shows my resilience. It does not mean my original plan was a bad one."

How has a change of plans strengthened your company?

_____

_____

_____

_____

_____

_____

_____

_____

_____

_____

_____

_____

Repeat the Affirmation of the Day.

DAY 99

My Affirmation of the Day

"I am stronger than I was yesterday and only half as strong as I will be tomorrow."

Highlight your strengths.

_____

_____

_____

_____

_____

_____

_____

_____

_____

_____

_____

_____

_____

Repeat the Affirmation of the Day.

DAY 100

My Affirmation of the Day

"Nothing is impossible. I will find a way!"

What tools and strategies do you have when challenges arise?

_____

_____

_____

_____

_____

_____

_____

_____

_____

_____

_____

_____

Repeat the Affirmation of the Day.

10 Day Check-Up

How has your mindset shifted about your business in the past 10 days?

Write about the progress you have made in the past ten days. Remember each day you work on your business goals is a day of progress. Also, identify what you want to accomplish in the upcoming ten days and the actions you will take to make these short-term goals your reality.

_____

_____

_____

_____

_____

_____

_____

_____

_____

_____

_____

_____

_____

_____

_____

_____

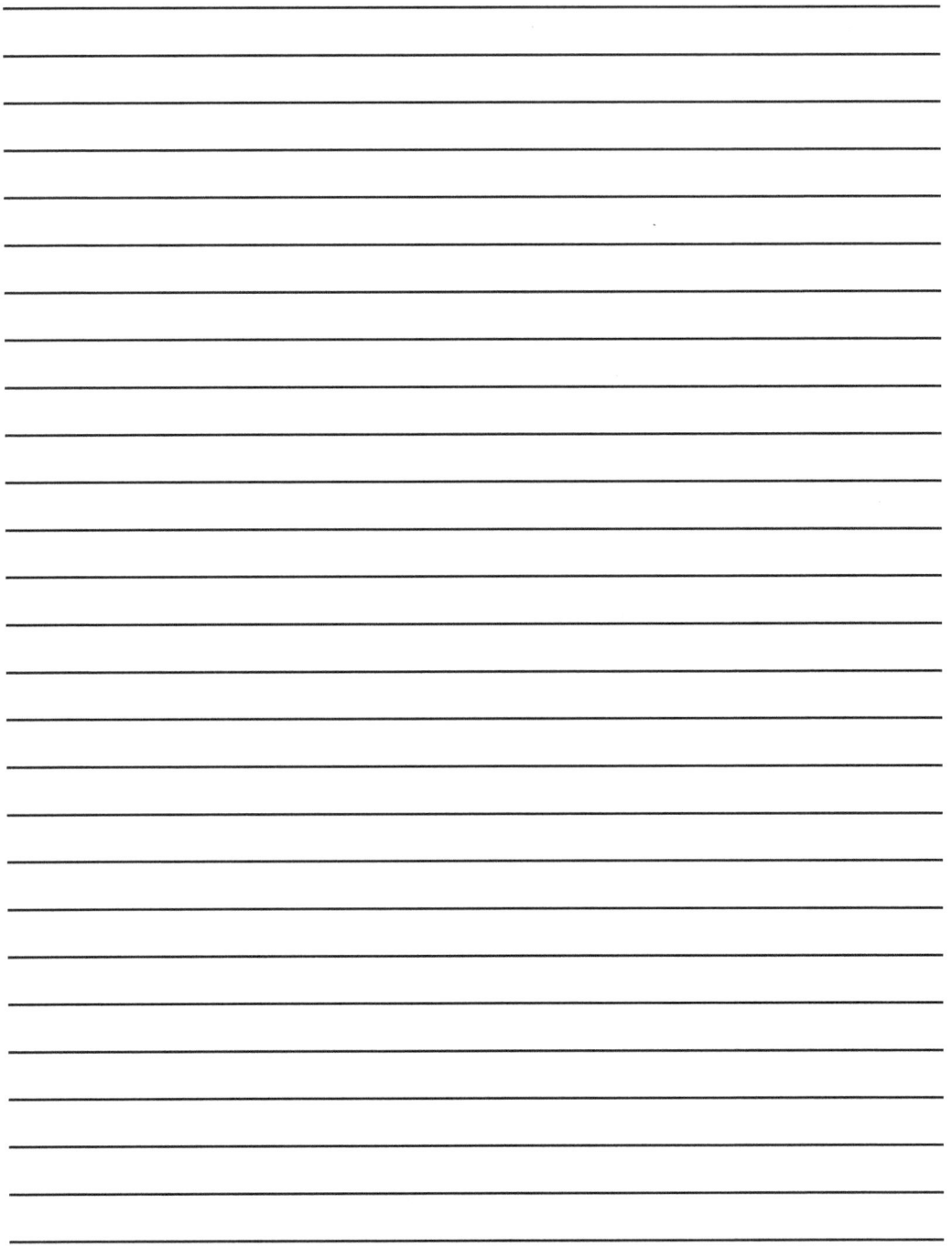

Your Next 100 Days

You have completed 100 days of speaking positively about yourself and your business. You have been intentional with your thoughts and actions.

What have you learned on this journey?

How did your business transform?

_____
_____
_____
_____
_____
_____
_____
_____
_____
_____

What are your goals for the next 100 days?

_____
_____
_____
_____
_____
_____
_____
_____
_____
_____

MONTH _____

SUNDAY	MONDAY	TUESDAY	WEDNESDAY	THURSDAY	FRIDAY	SATURDAY

Notes

MONTH _____

SUNDAY	MONDAY	TUESDAY	WEDNESDAY	THURSDAY	FRIDAY	SATURDAY

Notes

MONTH _____

SUNDAY	MONDAY	TUESDAY	WEDNESDAY	THURSDAY	FRIDAY	SATURDAY

Notes

MONTH _____

SUNDAY	MONDAY	TUESDAY	WEDNESDAY	THURSDAY	FRIDAY	SATURDAY

Notes

MONTH _____

SUNDAY	MONDAY	TUESDAY	WEDNESDAY	THURSDAY	FRIDAY	SATURDAY

Notes

MONTH _____

SUNDAY	MONDAY	TUESDAY	WEDNESDAY	THURSDAY	FRIDAY	SATURDAY

Notes

MONTH _____

SUNDAY	MONDAY	TUESDAY	WEDNESDAY	THURSDAY	FRIDAY	SATURDAY

Notes

MONTH _____

SUNDAY	MONDAY	TUESDAY	WEDNESDAY	THURSDAY	FRIDAY	SATURDAY

Notes

MONTH _____

SUNDAY	MONDAY	TUESDAY	WEDNESDAY	THURSDAY	FRIDAY	SATURDAY

Notes

MONTH _____

SUNDAY	MONDAY	TUESDAY	WEDNESDAY	THURSDAY	FRIDAY	SATURDAY

Notes

MONTH _____

SUNDAY	MONDAY	TUESDAY	WEDNESDAY	THURSDAY	FRIDAY	SATURDAY

Notes

MONTH _____

SUNDAY	MONDAY	TUESDAY	WEDNESDAY	THURSDAY	FRIDAY	SATURDAY

Notes

www.ingramcontent.com/pod-product-compliance
Lightning Source LLC
Chambersburg PA
CBHW062039090426
42740CB00016B/2952